To Hear the Rain

To Hear the Rain

Selected Haiku of Peggy Lyles

Randy M. Brooks, Editor
Lidonna Beer, Student Editor

Brooks Books
Decatur, Illinois

Publication Credits

Grateful acknowledgment is made to the editors of the following publications in which some of these poems appeared in present or earlier versions: *Acorn; Bottom Dog Press; Brussels Sprout; Chiyo's Corner; Cicada* (Canada); *Climbing the Flame Tree* (The New Zealand Poetry Society, Inc. 1998); *Daybreak; Dragonfly; Favorite Haiku, H. F Noyes, Volumes 2, 3, and 5* (Red Moon Press, 1999, 2000, 2002); *Frogpond; Global Haiku: Twenty-five Poets World-wide* (Iron Press, 2000); *Haiga Online; haijinx; A Haiku Alphabet in Celebration of Fall* (Proof Press 1996); *The Haiku Anthology, 2nd and 3rd editions* (Simon and Schuster 1986; W. W. Norton & Co., Inc.,1999 and 2000); *Haiku Canada Press; Haiku Compass; The Haiku Handbook* (McGraw-Hill,1985; Kondansha, 1996); *Haiku Light; Haiku Moment* (Tuttle, 1993); *A Haiku Path* (HSA, 1994); *Haiku Quarterly; Haiku World* (Kondansha, 1989); *The Heron's Nest; Heron Quarterly; High/Coo Press; High/Coo Quarterly; Hummingbird; The Illinois Times; In Buddha's Temple; Japan Airlines Anthology* (1988); *Ko; Like a Summer Peach* (Papier Mache Press, 1996); *The Mainichi Daily News; The Mainichi Shimbun; Mayfly; Mirrors; Modern Haiku; New Cicada; New World Poetry Bi-Monthly; Northeast; Outch; Persimmon, The Red Moon Anthology* (1998, 1999, 2000); *The Rise and Fall of Sparrows* (Los Hombres Press 1990); *Saki Press; Short and Sweet* (Penguin Books 1993); *Skylark* (India); *Snapshots; Snapshot Press; Solares Hill; South by Southeast; Swamp Press; Tightrope; Tundra; Wind Chimes Quarterly; Wind Chimes Press; The Windless Orchard; Woodnotes;The World Haiku Review; The World Haiku Wall; The Writer; The Writer's Market.*

Publishers' Note

Brooks Books is pleased to publish *To Hear the Rain: Selected Haiku of Peggy Lyles*, in the Goodrich Haiku Masters series. Each book in this series includes the very best haiku by an author who has spent a significant portion of his or her life's work in this genre. It is our hope that readers will enjoy these top-quality haiku and develop an appreciation for each author's contributions to the growth of haiku in English.

Special thanks are due to the several readers who have reviewed, evaluated and assisted the editors with the selection of the haiku to be included in this book.

Several accomplished haiku writers and editors reviewed this body of writing—evaluating and responding with selections of favorite haiku they recommended be included in the final book. These enthusiastic readers have provided a valuable service, and it is our pleasure to publicly thank them for their assistance. The readers for this collection include: Bill Pauly, Christopher Herold, Lee Gurga, Ellen Compton, Ferris Gilli, John Stevenson, Pamela Miller Ness, Tom Clausen and Emiko Miyashita.

Also, special thanks to Lidonna Beer, a Millikin University student editor intern with Brooks Books in the spring of 2000. Lidonna admired Peggy Lyles' work and interviewed her for a research project in the Global Haiku Traditions course. Part of this interview is included in the appendix.

Randy & Shirley Brooks
Decatur, Illinois
September 7, 2002

Printed in the United States of America

First edition available only in
library clothbound binding.

ISBN: 1-929820-03-8

Brooks Books
3720 N. Woodridge Drive
Decatur, Illinois 62526

http://www.familynet.net/~brooksbooks
email: brooksbooks@q-com.com

Table of Contents

Author's Preface 9

Preface 12
by Christopher Herold

Haiku 17

Appendix

About the Author 121

Author's Haiku Awards 123

Interview with the Author 125
by Lidonna Beer

dedicated to

Bill
and our family

Author's Preface: Sharing the Open Secret

"A haiku is an open secret."
—Robert Spiess (1921-2002)

"Sharing is one of the things we want most in life, to give something of ourselves to others, so that they might accept us and our experiences and perceptions as important. The haiku, while short, is long enough to give others an impression of who we are, some piece of the story of our lives. Yet it does not go on forever, like a self-indulgent autobiography, without getting to the point. And it leaves room for a response, so the sharing can become mutual."
—William J. Higginson
The Haiku Handbook

"Haiku is basically about living with intense awareness, about having an openness to the existence around us—a kind of openness that involves seeing, hearing, smelling, tasting, and touching."
—Cor van den Heuvel
The Haiku Anthology, 3rd edition

Sometimes we say too much. Words get in the way. Abstractions cloak perceptions and dull communication about real things. No wonder haiku are so popular all around the world. Brief and immediate they compress significant observations, experiences, and insights into images that engage the senses and feelings. I think of them as open-ended and open-handed poems, capable of receiving, being, and giving all at once. Expressed in simple language, they invite the reader to participate as co-creator. Sometimes they seem to leap from heart to heart.

Like the great epics, haiku always begin "in the middle of things." Unlike other literature, they stop in the space of a human breath, forming vibrant crystals ready to reactivate the tones of a moment's experience. A good haiku offers just enough words, just the right words, to recreate the essence of a specific time and place and hold it permanently available. If tingles of heightened awareness inform the poet and the moment, they are likely to excite similar responses in a receptive reader, so that the haiku expands and resonates.

Compression and the energy it produces are characteristic of all poetry. So is careful diction with close attention to the denotations, connotations, and associative possibilities of words. Sound enhances meaning. Every nuance contributes to the total effect. Haiku's extreme brevity makes all these qualities especially important to its successful creation. More intuitive than intellectual, haiku rarely depend upon simile, metaphor, or other tropes. Instead, juxtaposed images suggest internal comparisons and allow for layers of meaning. Haiku can be accessible and deep, immediate and enduring. They are about life, and my life is richer because of them.

I value the insight and pleasure excellent haiku poets have given me. Whether from seventeenth-century Japan or twenty-first-century Romania, they speak clearly and intimately of real things and convey universal human feelings. I believe that haiku's influence on twentieth-century American poetry was far greater than has yet been understood, and that it has already become the primary "people's poetry" worldwide.

The vital interaction among haiku poets creates a fertile environment for expression and development. For years, I have thought of English-language haiku as literature poets are creating together. Fine anthologies show the range and achievement of the "haiku movement," and a steadily growing number of excellent collections by individual authors offer extended glimpses of specific lives.

Now I am glad to share the best of my own haiku, written over almost twenty-five years. I do so with gratitude for the experiences, revelations, and relationships they celebrate and thankful pleasure in having written them.

How would I want you to read these pieces of the story of my life?

Slowly.

Individually.

More than once.

Preferably aloud.

Above all, I want you to read them with assurance of their essential honesty, and faith that what you find in them is what they mean and are. I hope the poems link to your sensory perceptions and affirm a connection between what Robert Frost called inner and outer weather. I hope they touch your sense of wonder, stirring responses that make the sharing mutual. I hope they spark the desire, new or renewed, to write and share your own haiku. Yes, much is left out. That is the way of haiku. The omissions leave room for each reader to become part of the experience and to take the haiku to whatever breadth and depth he discovers. That is how the open secret spreads.

—Peggy Lyles
Tucker, Georgia
May 27, 2002

Preface: The Vibrant Haiku of Peggy Lyles

Are you an old hand at English language haiku? Well-versed in its history and literature? Aware of the myriad debates about what makes a haiku a haiku? Or are you a relative newcomer to this unique form of expression, impressed by the way so few words convey so much vitality? Intuiting that there is much more to be discovered beneath the surface of words? Experienced or not, I feel certain that you'll be smitten by what you find in this magnificent collection, selected from among the many poems written by Peggy Willis Lyles during the past twenty-five years. So, forget what you know; don't worry about what you don't know. Simply immerse yourself in these vibrant moments.

Peggy Lyles is one of our most highly regarded English language haiku poets, and for good reason. She is finely attuned to her surroundings, and when she gives expression to her experiences of the world around her, she is utterly honest. As I read her poems I know full well that there is no contrivance, that I have not been manipulated. Lyles doesn't pad her haiku with unnecessary words, nor does she strip them down to the point of being inaccessible. She sustains her focus on the experiences that inspire her, thereby gaining better understanding of them. When it comes time to translate those experiences into poems, she finds uncomplicated words and natural syntax to reveal her discoveries as clearly as possible. In other words, while Lyles keeps to the truth of her experiences, she doesn't forget her readers. She's adept in the art of communication. Because her craft appears effortless, we are readily engaged by her words, and drawn into the essential nature of those things that inspired her.

Lyles has another special gift. She is quick to recognize connections. Not only does she see how material things are connected, she recognizes that those things that we perceive outwardly are actually extensions of our inner atmosphere, our human condition. Through expert use of juxtaposition, Lyles' haiku consistently bring about the spontaneous insights that are a hallmark of haiku. How many haiku have you read that feature a dentist's lead apron, or human cloning? In connection with a fast-breaking news report, the lead apron immediately gains dramatic significance. The observance of falling snowflakes takes place during a discussion of human cloning. Instantly we are faced with paradox—within our sameness we are different; within our differences we are the same.

An important tenet in the world of haiku is "Show, don't tell." Lyles is a master at this. She calls attention to something in particular without ever naming it. Sometimes it's an object, for instance the sky in:

> bare branches
> I choose a layer
> of blue silk

Sometimes an emotion, like the empathic ache in:

> lingering heat
> the third-grade classroom
> one desk short

All the seats in a classroom have been taken. The last child to enter is left standing. What third-grader wouldn't be embarrassed to stand out in such a way?

My love of music propelled me into making a career as a percussionist. That same love led me beyond musical instruments. There's music in everything, haiku included. Music plays an important role in rendering a haiku effective. The poems in this collection have marvelous rhythm and lilt. Read any of them aloud. Read all of them aloud! Not only is the diction natural, the very sounds of the words enhance the poet's experience.

These haiku portray a person who has a profound appreciation for the musicality of language. That these poems are pleasing to the ear gives me confidence in the person who composed them. I feel safe to explore deeply. I am willing to follow Lyles to the heart of each of her inspired moments. Take for instance:

Mother's scarf
slides from my shoulder
wild violets

Such sibilance! And the assonance of the long "i" sounds, even the relationship of the "m"s (both in sound and in their family connection) are in concordance. How easy it is to plumb the depths of nostalgia in this poem. Just as music evokes mood and calls forth our emotions, so too do these haiku. Listen to them.

Lyles is keenly aware of each of the other senses as well. A bee is enough to stir up the scent of apple mint. In another poem, vinegar-soaked cucumbers make me salivate, especially once the final line establishes how hot the day is. Those cucumbers then serve to cool me as well. You will often find combinations of sensory stimuli in a single haiku. While a mayfly bumps against a screen, the poet squeezes warm beets from their skins (sound, touch, color). Directly or indirectly, you will find that this collection is especially tactile.

I find it difficult to use the medium of haiku when expressing myself about romantic love, almost always opting to slip into tanka or some other form of expression. Lyles, however, manages this trick beautifully:

wind and rain
the hand I reach for
in the dark

Two other prominent themes that come into Lyles' haiku are the dynamics of family and delight with children. It is obvious to me that these are of utmost importance in Lyles' life, more even than her passion for writing—more than haiku. Her family haiku are born of love—lots of it. Two such poems:

teaching her to sew . . .
I wind back to bobbin thread
from half a life ago

and

for her mother
bluets
roots and all

The haiku in this book are far more than skillfully recreated scenes or beautiful snapshots. The combinations of images presented create openings to ambient moods and emotions. There is a sense of gentleness in the power that pervades these moods. Gentleness. Another of Lyles' great strengths. As I mentioned earlier, she is finely attuned to the connection between feelings and surroundings. This sort of sensitivity demands great courage, the courage to be vulnerable.

Lyles' haiku often achieve the quality of interpenetration about which R. H. Blyth wrote: "At the moment of composition or appreciation, there is no distinction between inner and outer. Life runs so freely between them that we perceive things by introspection, and our experiences of the 'outer' world have the same immediacy, validity and certainty as have states of pure 'self' consciousness."

I have been reading and marveling over Peggy Lyles' haiku since the early 1980's. In recent years we have become friends through correspondence and writing renku together. In our communication I feel welcome, a part of Peggy's extended family. I know others who also feel this way. There is something very special about Peggy Willis Lyles. She makes of herself a well-polished mirror and what I see in this mirror pleases me. Thank you Peggy, for your wisdom and for your generous and accepting nature. They shine brilliantly throughout this collection of haiku.

—Christopher Herold
Port Townsend, Washington
July 20, 2002

haze-blurred horizon . . .
a painted bunting hovers
in the sea oats' curve

the third-note rise
of a towhee's song
fragrant breeze

a damp fern
strokes my ankle
dark eyes of the doe

offertory chant:
in the darkened vestibule
umbrellas drip

for her mother
bluets
roots and all

hazy moon
the nun begins her journey
with a backward glance

an open window
somewhere
a woman's wordless song

a mayfly
taps the screen—
warm beets slip their skins

summer stillness
the play of light and shadow
on the windchimes

shimmering pines
a taste of the mountain
from your cupped hands

country church
the summer smell of cotton
freshly ironed

sweet peas
tremble on the trellis
the bride's "I will"

sun shower
the river otter
somersaults

through a maze of lilies brushstrokes of the trout

cheek on her hand
. . . the pages
turn themselves

lightning flash
the brass quintet
tuning up

smooth garden bench
a woman embroiders
a unicorn

dew drops
on the dark rose
our reflections

lingering heat
the third-grade classroom
one desk short

family graveyard
a boy finds his middle name
on the oldest stone

October twilight
the scarecrow in the garden
drops its other glove

piano lesson
her braids outdo
the metronome

chalk dust
in the eraser trough
autumn chill

yellow leaves
a girl plays hopscotch
by herself

first frost . . .
on a silver card tray
wild persimmons

bare branches
I choose a layer
of blue silk

snowflake
against cold glass
cat’s paw

noon whistle . . .
icicles dripping
splintered light

winter night
a spark between the tweeds
of strangers

starlight
on the harp strings
Christmas Eve

the first notes
squeezed from bagpipes
small town parade

the baby
reaches for his father's breath
mallards on the lake

tea fragrance
from an empty cup
the thin winter moon

bread rising
yellow crocuses
fill with snow

moving day
the dogwood tree
in full white bloom

six moon shells
where the neap tide turned . . .
I hear your heart

warm sea
we swim into phosphorescence
lightly touching

Beethoven's ninth
raindrops bounce
from cobblestones

a maple seed
floats on the millpond . . .
deep blue sky

oval frame
a woman curves
around her child

summer night
we turn out all the lights
to hear the rain

Gershwin's lullaby
magnolia petals ladle
fireflies

turtle through the reeds
whispering
our secrets

good morning kiss
wing beats
of the hummingbird

mother-daughter
small talk
snap beans

cucumbers
soaked in vinegar—
the heat

I shake the vase
a bouquet of red roses
finds its shape

quivering heat
a wasp slips from the flowers
hidden in the fig

long twilight
at the woman's ear
a small pearl glows

feverish child
shadowing the night light
a luna moth

cicadas
workmen on a scaffold
sanding off old paint

thunderheads pass . . .
a blue jay bathing
in the dust

aperitifs
the sunflower's shadow
reaches her silk blouse

city heat
a boy stirs oily rainbows
with his pocket knife

starry night
the telescope
wobbles

moon
and melon cooling
with us in the stream

Saturday
he whistles as he turns
the children's pancakes

three odd socks
in the wicker basket—
autumn rain

traffic jam
my small son asks
who made God

graveside rain . . .
the old hymn fading
into earth scent

a doe's leap
darkens the oyster shell road
twilight

lunch at the zoo
even among gorillas
some who sit apart

short of the crest
the jogger breaks his stride
red leaves in the air

clay on the wheel I confess my faith

cedar shavings
the carpenter's magnet
snaps up tacks

marsh lights
the owl's cry dilates
our eyes

witnessing his will
the frost-hatched
pane

bitter wind . . .
the hand that cups the flame
aglow

snowed in
the wedding-ring quilt
lumpy with children

winter night
he patiently untangles
her antique silver chain

teaching her to sew . . .
I wind back to bobbin thread
from half a life ago

midnight
the cat walks
up piano keys

into the night
we talk of human cloning
            snowflakes

dawn light
on white camellias
the fever breaks

watermark
    the way the master's brush
strokes wings

attic sun
from Grandmother's gown
a grain of rice

buds swell
a woman beats her dust mop
against an old brick wall

cathedral garden
cardinals in the birdbath
scatter drops of light

first warm day
two left gloves
for gardening

the boy stands still
fingers splayed
above a starfish

chasing butterflies . . .
the girl with Wednesday's ashes
on her brow

no thought
of air until
that blue feather's drift

plants move
beneath the pond's dark surface
scattered stars

birdsong
through open windows—
he lifts the veil

passion flower
your faith
or mine?

river baptism
another frog
with just three legs

clouds gathering
the crowned whelk twirled
into itself

distant jazz
a calla lily
catches rain

bird song
lost
in bird song

dust on the pews
afternoon sun washes
an apostle's feet

lingering good-byes . . .
hard rye crusts on a paper plate
beside the radish rose

night flight
a young man fast asleep
beside his cello

sonic boom
the peony sheds
a small black ant

fast-breaking news
weight of the lead apron
in the dentist's chair

thunderclap
the frayed shoestring
snaps

dress by dress
the story of her life
day lilies close

cross current—
in the cooler
blue crabs fight

thunderheads offshore
the osprey coming early
to its nest

crescent moon
a periscope rises
from the oil spill

reaching for green pears—
the pull
of an old scar

dragonfly . . .
the tai chi master
shifts his stance

high noon
a cat stares down
the chipmunk's hole

crunch of frost
the dollmaker twists
a corn-shuck man

wild persimmons
a woman at the roadside
wiggles her last tooth

nip of fall . . .
a rabbit's tooth marks
in magnolia leaves

soft Gullah
at the graveside . . .
blue glass shines

delta autumn
the storyteller cradles
his gun

stillness
in the storm's eye
stars

recycling—
before he grinds the stump
he counts the rings

I brush
my mother's hair
the sparks

a handprint
on the hospice window
fingers widely spread

processional
cold wind lifts one corner
of the pall

dinner party
glancing up from grace
to the flood mark on the wall

black-water pond
reflections lapping
cypress knees

wind and rain
the hand I reach for
in the dark

ice flecks
on azalea buds
the koi go deep

gray morning
the weight of mist
in Spanish moss

downpour
a whelk's foot stretches
toward the waves

damp earth smell
of the unglazed bowl
the potter breathes

before we knew its name the indigo bunting

still at the edge
of its shadow—
the frog

deep chords
from the practice room
a bee stirs apple mint

Mother's scarf
slides from my shoulder
wild violets

spring sunbeam
the baby’s toes
spread apart

honeysuckle
    we open jelly jars
    for fireflies

glide of the kayak
ripples overlapping
water lilies

boarding call
the ripe banana flavor
of the small one's cheek

the tide's shape
in bent cord grass
fiddler crabs

first star
the leaf that shed a raindrop
springing back

brief visit
peony open
to its heart

lights out
. . . the firefly
inside

wing beats
in the chimney
the short night

a black bear
noses muscadines
slow summer stream

mayflies
spin between us
a lost thought

an old song
in our second language
starry night

amber light
creased in a roadmap
a place we've been

fallow field
in one flash the redbird
and the wish

autumn sea
a little girl's love
of small brown shells

through the doe's ear
sunset
flickers

cricket sounds
rise into night
the names of the dead

Indian summer
a turtle on a turtle
on a rock

November mist
wood smoke scents
the jogger's way

a strong draft
as you enter
embers glow

level ground
over leaves
Grandmother's quilt

green reach
of amaryllis
slanting sun

winter solstice
our son reads a fairy tale
to his unborn child

dog-eared script
I prompt a wise man
from the wings

I rinse the rice
a second time
New Year's Day

About the Author

Peggy Willis Lyles was born in Summerville, South Carolina, on September 17, 1939. Now she and her husband, Bill, live in Tucker, Georgia, a suburb of Atlanta, and often visit Charleston and the surrounding South Carolina Lowcountry, where she grew up.

She attended the College of Charleston and The Citadel, graduated with honors from Columbia College, and received her MA degree in English from Tulane University, where she was a Woodrow Wilson Fellow for 1960-61. As a graduate student, she taught classes in freshman English at Sophie Newcomb College. Later she taught at High Point High School and High Point College in North Carolina. Her daughter and son were born in Charleston, SC, in the mid-sixties. The family moved to Athens, Georgia, in 1968 and lived there for 18 years.

Although complications of Crohn's disease interrupted and eventually curtailed Lyles's academic career, she taught at the University of Georgia, and, as a volunteer, led creative writing workshops for elementary, middle, and high school students. For five years she was poetry editor of the regional magazine *Georgia Journal*.

Reading Cor van den Heuvel's *The Haiku Anthology*, first edition, convinced her of the freshness, sparkle, and value of English-language haiku. That enthusiasm has led to considerable study of classic and contemporary Japanese haiku and to involvement in the haiku movement worldwide.

Since the late 1970's her work has been published regularly in leading journals in the United States and abroad. She has received awards from *Modern Haiku, Wind Chimes, Woodnotes, Mayfly, The Heron's Nest*, the Haiku Society of America, the Museum of Haiku Literature, Snapshot Press, the *Mainichi Daily News*, Japan Airlines, the New Zealand Poetry Society, the Suruga Baika Literary Festival, *The People's Poetry Newsletter*, Haiku Poets of Northern California, the World Haiku Club, and other publications and organizations. She has judged competitions for the Haiku Society of America, the North Carolina Haiku Association, the Poetry Society of Georgia, the Tallahassee Writer's Association, and other groups.

Beginning with the September 2002 issue, Lyles is an associate editor of the on-line and print journal, *The Heron's Nest*.

She and her partners Ferris Gilli and Paul MacNeil won Grand Prize for their kasen renku "Castle Tour" in the 2000 Bernard Einbond Renku contest sponsored by the Haiku Society of America and second place in the same contest in 2001. She has also received awards for rengay written with partners Lori Laliberte-Carey and Mitzi Trout and with Ferris Gilli and Juanito Escareal.

A long-term member of the Haiku Society of America and a founding member of Pinecone, the North Georgia Haiku Society, she has read her poetry at Haiku Chicago 1995; the Global Haiku Festival, Millikin University 2000; and Haiku North America, Boston 2001; as well as in classrooms, bookstores, and clubrooms.

Her previously published collections include:

> *Red Leaves in the Air* (High/Coo Press, 1979)
>
> *Still at the Edge* (Swamp Press, 1980)
>
> *Prisms*, a Wind Chimes Haiku Sheet, 1986
>
> *Thirty-Six Tones*, (Saki Press, 2001)
> a Virgil Hutton haiku chapbook award
> winner for 2000-2001

Award Credits

"for her mother" .... (p. 19)
runner-up for *The Snapshot Haiku Calendar* 2003.

"sun shower" .... (p. 26)
highly commended in the 1998 New Zealand International Haiku Competition.

"October twilight" .... (p. 31)
10th Anniversary Merit Award and The Clement Hoyt Memorial Award from *Modern Haiku*, X:3, Autumn 1979.

"piano lesson" .... (p. 32)
first place for senryu in the 1999 San Francisco International Haiku, Senryu, and Tanka Competition.

"Gershwin's lullaby" .... (p. 46)
Mayfly's Best-of-Issue Haiga Award for #30, Winter 2001.

"I shake the vase" .... (p. 49)
Editors' Choice Honorable Mention in *Woodnotes* #13, Summer 1992.

"long twilight" .... (p. 50)
first prize in the 1989 *Mainichi Daily News* Contest.

"lunch at the zoo" .... (p. 59)
Best-of-Issue Award from *Modern Haiku* for XXXIII:1, Winter/Spring 2001.

"short of the crest," .... (p. 60)
in an earlier version, 3rd place in the *Dragonfly Quarterly* Contest for October 1978.

"marsh lights" .... (p. 62)
Honorable Mention in the 1987 *Mainichi Daily News* Contest.

"bitter wind" .... (p. 63)
Museum of Haiku Literature Award, *Frogpond* VII:4, 1985.

"teaching her to sew . . ." .... (p. 66)
Honorable Mention Award from *Modern Haiku* for XII:1, Winter/Spring 1981.

"watermark" .... (p. 68)
Honorable Mention in the 1987-88 Japan Air Lines Contest.

"chasing butterflies" .... (p. 73)
Special Mention Award from *Modern Haiku*, XI:2, 1980.

"no thought" .... (p. 74)
theme haiku for *Frogpond* XX:1, May 1997.

"birdsong" .... (p. 75)
Honorable Mention in the Haiku Society of America's Harold H. Henderson Contest for 1986.

"thunderclap" .... (p. 82)
the *Woodnotes* Award for # 27, Winter 1995.

"dragonfly . . ." .... (p. 87)
The Heron's Nest Award for II:11, November 2000, and *the Heron's Nest* Valentine Award (Reader's Choice) for 2000.

"high noon" .... (p. 88)
Editors' Choice for *The Heron's Nest*, II:1, January 2001.

"I brush" .... (p. 93)
Museum of Haiku Literature Award *Frogpond* XXI:2, 1998.

"gray morning" .... (p. 98)
The Heron's Nest Award for IV:3, March 2002.

"downpour" .... (p. 98)
runner-up for *The Snapshot Haiku Calendar* 2001.

"Mother's scarf" .... (p. 102)
March winner for *The Snapshot Haiku Calendar* 2003.

"spring sunbeam" .... (p. 103)
first prize for haiku in the World Haiku Festival 2000 Poetry Competition, and was the April and Spring winner for *The Snapshot Haiku Calendar* 2000.

"lights out" .... (p. 108)
honorable mention in the Haiku Society of America's Harold H. Henderson Memorial Contest for 1980.

"a black bear" .... (p. 109)
honorable mention in the Loke Hilikimani contest for 1990.

"November mist" .... (p. 116)
The *Woodnotes* Award for #18, 1993.

"I rinse the rice" .... (p. 119)
January winner for *The Snapshot Haiku Calendar* 2003.

An interview with Peggy Willis Lyles

by Lidonna Beer
April 2000

Where does your inspiration for haiku come from?

Lyles: Usually from the sensory experiences that surround everyday life—the tastes, smells, textures, sounds and sights of the world close at hand. Sometimes I simply report what I experience, such as a towhee's song coinciding with a fragrant breeze or sleet with an eclipse of the moon. Such natural juxtapositions stir physical and emotional responses in me and are poems ripe for the taking.

At other times memory plays a part or a particular emotion that triggers an active search for concrete details to convey it. I think there is a nice paradox in haiku: the poet brings her whole life's experience, everything she is, to each one, and at the same time virtually disappears into the details of the poem's moment. At best, haiku merge images from the exterior world with the landscape of the poet's heart so effectively that a receptive and fully participatory reader can become part of the poem, too.

When did you begin writing haiku?

Lyles: I published some uninformed attempts in *Haiku Highlights* and a few other little magazines in the mid-Sixties. Later, the first edition of Cor van den Heuvel's *The Haiku Handbook,* which I found in the University of Georgia Bookstore in 1976, brought me firmly into the North American haiku movement. The haiku there still sparkle with vitality and create ever-widening ripples. The poems thrilled me with a "shock of recognition." Something fine was in progress, and references to books and contemporary haiku magazines offered first steps toward becoming part of it.

Do you have a mentor, someone who introduced you to haiku or had the most influence on your style?

Lyles: I think of many haiku poets as mentors at a distance, usually teaching me through their work rather than by specific instruction. Perceptive editors, Robert Spiess in particular, have given me invaluable guidance simply by accepting some haiku and returning others.

How often do you participate in conferences and other haiku gatherings?

Lyles: I attended Haiku Chicago in 1995 and the Global Haiku Festival at Millikin. In addition I meet bi-monthly with a small group of haiku enthusiasts here in the Atlanta area.

How do you edit your haiku?

Lyles: Unsystematically. Sometimes repeatedly, sometimes slightly, sometimes hardly at all. Some of the best ones have claimed their right words immediately, becoming what they are in a breath's space. Other times a phrase or a pair of lines stays in a notebook for a very long time, waiting for the rest of the poem to show up. Not long ago, in the process of writing to another poet about a storm he had recently experienced, I recalled the first two lines of an eleven-year-old haiku that had never felt finished. No wonder. A hurricane changed the landscape just after I jotted the images. The "right" third line—simply "the wind"—was not part of the initial experience; it was the completion of the haiku as I re-experienced it in a new context.

Technically, revisions usually involve omitting unnecessary words and sharpening word choice, rearranging lines, and bringing the sound of the poem closer to its sense. Sometimes I change the focal distance, usually moving in closer, occasionally backing off for a wider view. Often I try to "go back to the moment" to decide whether I have included the best details to shape it into a poem.

Rewording to avoid confusion is important, too. Reading the haiku aloud is part of the process for me—and setting new haiku aside to re-evaluate after a "cooling off" period.

What do you think about reading haiku out loud?

Lyles: I find reading aloud an essential step in the process of composition, and highly recommend it for the individual wanting a full experience of someone else's haiku. The sound of words always matters.

A long round of oral presentations, though, can strain the most receptive audience. That scenario, I believe, is best confined to haiku conferences where enthusiasts are getting to know each other and especially value the opportunity to hear poets reading their work.

For more general audiences, a carefully paced, relatively brief selection of haiku, each surrounded by adequate silence and perhaps read twice, can be vivid and moving. Experiments combining haiku with other art forms, music and dance as well as painting, really intrigue me. I would especially like to see some fine filmmakers experiment with a montage presentation of haiku and images, maybe involving readers other than the authors.

I love the sound of words, the varied rhythms of human speech. As more and more haiku readings occur and the poets compare notes on what works well, I believe we will tap into ever better possibilities. I hope so. For the moment, I think of haiku less as presentation poetry than as tiny word pictures for individual readers to experience and savor.